SEAGULLS WHITE AS EVER

Wayne F. Burke

ISBN: 978-81-8253-874-0

First Edition: 2022
Rs. 200/-

Cyberwit.net
HIG 45 Kaushambi Kunj, Kalindipuram
Allahabad - 211011 (U.P.) India
http://www.cyberwit.net
Tel: +(91) 9415091004
E-mail: info@cyberwit.net

Contents

CITY

squat fire hydrant
does not speak
and neither does
the tall lamp post—
only the chunky mailbox, with big
yapper-mouth,
says anything at all.

5 PM

Friday afternoon, and
the crush of traffic through
downtown streets,
cars and buses, roar of
trucks Bang
Boom
the gurgle of a motorsuckle—
everyone headed home
or who knows where (I don't)
I wish everyone would tone it down
but, fat chance
of that, I know;
a seagull overhead, and
white as ever, does not
seem to mind the noise,
but I do.

Sun Shower

in the afternoon, a lone gray
trouble-making cloud
mid-sky;
the streets swamped and
sidewalks slick and
glistening in the
sunshine—
I look for a rainbow
but none to be seen; look
for the pot of gold, but
the sun has spent it
on the day,
her fierce gold eye cast
over the simmering land
until
dusk
when she dropped, dreaming
into the soft arms of spruce trees
along the ridge line.

City

I fell asleep while sitting on a bench
in the park
my head falling forward
until I woke
falling forward
waking
my head
for an hour
two hours
the sounds of the city
all around
though distant—
noisy city,
I silenced you.

Points

Pigeons circle in a pale blue
winter sky, their bellies and
wings glinting white
in afternoon sunshine.
Diamond points of chrome
and glass of
cars lined-up at the intersection
where east & west
greet north & south
and time is measured by
red, green and yellow lights…
The sun paints buildings
a whiter white, lights the
grass a brighter green, and
un-muddies brick,
while the intersection
sits
and pigeons circle
overhead.

No Charge

birds in white sky
darkling
over Burlington, Vermont
city by the lake;
tower chapels white and
pointed on the
college campuses,
dark birds over flat rooftops
overseen from 5-story
parking garage
where I lost my parking ticket
and could not find
I told the guy in the booth
he said "s'all right," and
let me go
no charge, I said "thank you"
and left under the yellow
arm.

Storm

A tornado on the
ridge line and
spreading clouds dark
as soot—
grumble of thunder
flash of lightening
and rain
drops big as grapes
splattering the parking lot
in a dance
of dervishes
I watch
from beneath the overhang
of
Armed Services Recruitment Center
where I stand
waiting it out—
the storm.

Dusk

Yellow sunset, baby blue sky:
granite statue of Robert Burns
stands twenty-five feet high
with his back to me—
church steeples
in his line of sight
and a jacket, which he will not need
tonight, in the crook of his arm.
Black darts of birds and
brown bricks, purple trees;
everything set
so it seems,
for night and slumber
for dusk to tuck the covers under
and lay to rest
even the best
of schemes.

sparkling granite curbstones
held in place by grout and dirt:
rocky constellations for
day-time star gazers

TRAIN

the train whistle calls me away
then returns me
to myself

Tremble

I am sitting by the
railroad tracks when
a train creeps past
with a groan from
the weight of
a granite load…
Creaking boxcars, and
iron squeal—
I tremble from the
crush of rock
on iron wheels,
grooved on tracks
worn smooth.

Train Song #1

The train rumbled
down the line
along steely resolve
of track and
across the back of
the groaning trestle—
the cannonball special—
hoot
hoot,
clack
clack,
a switch-back track
along the
sliding
side.

#2.

Train says
WHAAAT!
WHAAAT!
I watch it glide
by
and down the
track:
clickity-clack
clickity-clack,
and over the back
of the trestle.

CLOUD

the pigeons pirouette
through gray sky
slathered with
white clouds
like smoke
without
fire

Dark

dank
damp sky
and overhead clouds
like used dishrags
dripping
on red brick and
granite city; asphalt
sheen of
car headlights
in middle of a December
afternoon,
dulled by shades of
Northeast gray
and
by my mind
trudging through snow
that has yet
to arrive.

Clouds

I look to the clouds
for answers
but
do not find any
because
clouds are but phantoms
passing through, not
messages
written on a blue vault—
not signs,
or portents—
only vapor of
condensation, air-y
nothings, will-less
and
without even the substance
of a dream.

Great Gray Cloud

like an opened hand
and the sun,
a white disk,
creeping from
the gray into
blue space, and
becoming the
light of the world
again.

Blue Sky

white clouds
sun shining
on snow
and cars
driving by
but
no people
outside
because
twenty below zero
and colder
with the
wind chill;
a lone crow
riding the
wind currents
and a fluttering
leaf floating
down from
autumn to
die on the
winter ground.

New Day

Cloudy and overcast—
lush green grass
looks good enough to eat:
nut-sized buds on
trees, and green sweep
of the woods on
mountainsides under
chalk-white sky;
a blank slate
to write the story
of the day
upon.

Mirage

Late afternoon cloud vista
piled high, gray, black, and
white, with a rent
like a cavern of light
between clouds,
like a pathway to
Valhalla
that closes
after a huge gray pig
puts snout into the
hole and snuffs-up
all the light, though
the sun bleeds
through, and
now a blue pool
in the midst
like a mirage,
and two cuddle-fish
swimming side-by-side.

LEAVES

inverted umbrella of
a leaf
clinging to a rocking limb
in the yowl of a wind

A Dead Leaf

on the sidewalk
leaves an imprint then
slides away
to be dead
elsewhere,
among a heap
maybe
in rooftop gutter, or
cul de sac, or
other; else
to wander aimlessly
pushed hither and
thither (more hither) by the
wind, that
tore the leaf
from the tree
and brought it
to the sidewalk.

Fall

Last yellow leaves of the
season falling from the old
tree: grandmother-fingers of
tree limbs letting them go,
the leaves, dive-bombing,
slaloming, dropping like
acrobats on descent and
littering the ground where
they hop, wave, and
flop—pave a golden trail,
become mulch in the blades
of a lawnmower, or else
live to a rusty old age and
molder in the ground.

Forlorn

All the yellow leaves are
brown,
downed by wind and rain
and seasonal change:
they crackle underfoot
and listlessly roll,
moved by a breeze, and
go
skittering along, and
get stepped on, become
tattered, holed
like old shoes
even the Salvation Army
cannot use—
little forlorn-looking leaves,
ragged, lost
but returning
always
whence they came:
to mother
Earth.

SKY

the wind touches me
with cotton-tipped
fingers

A pigeon swoops in gray sky.
It is only the gray season, and
no reason for dread or
worry about
what is ahead; the same
as last year and the year before;
cold and colder, snow & ice, you
know the score, and
the end of the story
too.

Quetzalcoatl

A shimmering serpent curling
above the ridge line,
a golden eye in its head;
great hood out-spread—
vast spiral jetty of silver
feathers
begins to darken as
the underbelly of the
beast slithers
overhead
and brave birds
cross the sky
in solo flights.

6 PM and the
sun breaks through
an iron curtain of
clouds
and takes over the
sky,
brilliant gold-plated eye
gazing
as it has
since Earth began
as child of Chaos and
Serendipity,
nurtured by the
Milky Way,
and
later married to Sky
who begat Cloud
and Ocean.

Quack Quack

A duck flying solo across
the sky,
moving fast—
body like a vacuum cleaner bag,
barreling above telephone lines
glistening in sunshine
like the threads of a spider's web
hung tree to tree
one end the street to the
other—
barreling past a half-moon
like a cartoon smile
in blue sky
translucent
in last rays
of the sun.

SUN

warm sun, cold wind—
March into Spring

Glare

In the sun's glare
the black shadows
look solid
and the light
preternaturally stark, and
the sun herself
burning with unusual
ferocity, igniting
even the brown leaves of
trees, having a 2nd blooming
in October's
finale.

Sunset #5b

Pigeons lined-up on
a wire
below a flaming sun sinking
slow as cold molasses
down behind Pine Tree Ridge—
a passing seagull
noisily objects to
something, maybe
the presence of the
crow on top the telephone pole
(cawing an unlisted number).
The sun takes its sweet time
reaching the ridge line;
the crow swoops and
disappears in shadow;
the yellow sun sets the
ridge on fire
and dusk comes in
mellow.

Hillside

brown & gold in the
light of the
setting sun, not
one speck of snow left
from the storm
that blew in like the Wild West,
turning the landscape white
overnight, and
forcing me to dress
in heavy coat, hat and boots, and
to think and
stress about
what is coming
next
over the hillside.

Sunken Morning Sun

sucked into the miasma
of gray sky, shooting
last rays up through the
hollow sphere of it's
sinking, and
finally
being swallowed down the
mucky gullet and
smothered,
but coming out the quicksand
tunnel
and dropping through the
plaster of Paris sky,
until sealed from
view
again.

Nature

The sun in an encore
performance this
morning, turning
neon-green the
lawn next door, un-mown,
over-grown, left alone by
the new hippy-chick owner
letting nature have her
way…Good for her and
nature and me (no weed-
whacker bedlam to endure).
5 foot high pods at the
fence line looking
over into the Sodomite's yard
beyond, of sculpted grass,
garden, a Louie XVI scene
like at Versailles, sea
of flowers abounding on
the sward.

Sun & Moon

Great white shark floating
in the deep blue sea sky
gets vaporized by the
squid-eye of the sun
and becomes a school of
minnows nibbling at the
ridge line…
Meantime, the
moon like a snowball
somebody threw, and
it stuck,
about 500 yards up,
white-ly shining
in the blue
like
maybe it snowed there
last night.

SNOW

March snowstorm—
snow plows rumble, 3 AM
over roads of thought

Winter Story

White squiggles of tree limbs
after the snow storm—
a splurge of
asemic writing, telling
the tale of the forest
that the sprites, glittering
in the translucent air,
already know.

Iced-over car windows
for the scraping scraper,
a black-headed hoe-like
implement
plasticized,
kept on the
back seat
for handy usage
on cold days
in this hinterland
north of
most borders.

MISCELLANEOUS

dog days of August, muggy
with rain: some joker
with his lawn mower woke me
from a dream

Fly Paper

like yellow phlegm
in color, a sticky friend
hard to be rid of, hangs
around
from the ceiling, slightly
curled
like a lip; you wish
you had never reached-out to
it
once it sticks.
Now the task becomes
how to be rid of it.
How to detach and
quick before you get
hung-up too in a sticky
proposition you did not
bargain for—like being
free of a dog who
follows you home
because
you pet it
once.

Free

"Vermont the state with
no summer," wrote Louise
Gluck. Not much Spring
either, but the state has
something not every other
has, and that something is
plenty of ice cold water, as
much as anyone could want:
fill the tub, flood the basement,
cart barrels of it from the river,
give some to friends and
neighbors, spend it like
a drunken sailor: there is
more where it came from,
more in the making, the
state will never run out, and
it is FREE too.

The Parking Lot

lies flat,
silent—
nothing going on there
today,
except for parking,
same as on any other
day, same as
yesterday; different cars
maybe, but same places,
same décor too
of crushed cigarette butts
bottle caps
gum (stuck)
and oil stains that resemble
certain works of modern art.

Riverine

Gold sun, silver river
sparkle of crescents,
crinkles,
speckles;
aluminum ridges of rivulets
and ribbons unraveling
in procession
with gullied troughs
dark as licorice
and shadows of
silver birds
on mirror surface while
below,
fishes go
invisibly
about their business,
as above
the unseen heavens
flow.

Hot Enough

Waiting for the rain
on a sultry night in
summer after a steaming
day but the rain will not
come, only thunder, and
heat lightning, and
wind, that moves the
tree limbs, with a cool
breeze, but not cool
enough.

From out the hills
flows the River of Applause
that
downstream
becomes the River of Laughter
and giggles
and
wiggles under the
trestle
to the Bridge of Stone
and
beyond, where
the River of Silence
flows
into the River of Life
which goes
into River of Death.

www.ingramcontent.com/pod-product-compliance
Lightning Source LLC
Chambersburg PA
CBHW050026170726
48282CB00025B/563
9788182538740